Modern Karate

Modern Karate

**Steve Arneil
Bryan Dowler**

Contemporary Books, Inc.
Chicago

First published in England in 1974 by Kaye & Ward Ltd.
Published by Contemporary Books, Inc.
180 North Michigan Avenue, Chicago, Illinois 60601
Manufactured in the United States of America
Library of Congress Catalog Card Number: 80-65764
International Standard Book Number: 0-8092-8257-7 (cloth)
0-8092-8256-9 (paper)

CONTENTS

ACKNOWLEDGEMENTS

The authors wish to extend their sincere thanks and appreciation to Howard Collins, 3rd Dan, who kindly demonstrated many of the techniques shown in this book, and to Brian Bellingham who, at very short notice, took nearly all the photographs for this volume.

FOREWORD

The only way to judge a Karate Instructor is by his own talent and his ability to teach others to attain a high level of performance. In the same way this book can be evaluated only by the level of performance resulting from reading and studying its pages.

This book offers excellent form and good training procedures. I therefore suggest you add the necessary ingredient of yourself and make it work for you.

Ken Knudson, 5th Dan
President of the American Karate Association

WHAT IS KARATE?

The term *Karate* has been widely known and used in the western world for upwards of ten years. Whatever conception of Karate is held by the average man in the street, Karate has become in Western Europe and the United States as real a part of life in those ten years as Judo has become in the fifty years since its introduction. If Karate in the West continues to grow at anything like its recent rate, indications are that it will become a thoroughly integrated part of Western culture and, as with Judo, will be adapted by the occidental to suit his own particular physical and mental characteristics.

Fundamentally, Karate is an art or systematised method of bare-handed fighting. The word *Karate* itself literally translates as 'empty hand'. For some people Karate is also a way of life, and, for better or worse, increasingly a sport.

Although many of the hair-raising stories told about the legendary Karate masters can probably be dismissed as apocryphal, the authenticity of the abilities of the modern masters can be proved by the simple expedient of training under the masters or their accredited assistants, or by photographic proof. The abilities of experts from Japanese and Korean schools to split and break boards, stones, bricks and tiles with their bare hands and feet, and even with their heads, are now accepted. Nevertheless, there is an enormous difference between a static wooden board, a pile of bricks or tiles, and a bellicose lethal moving opponent, perhaps armed, who is determined to teach one the 'error of one's ways' once and for all.

It is to be regretted that, as an art, Karate is becoming 'westernised', that it stands in jeopardy of being prostituted in the eternal search for

I

Mammon. Doubtless the progression of Karate as a sport, which need have little reference to its more serious philosophical background, has opened the world of Karate to many more people, but it has also assisted many pseudo-experts in making their fortune – both orientals and occidentals. To those truly devoted to the Karate 'way', the rewards of the life itself are usually sufficient return.

There are numerous martial arts and even more numerous styles of Karate. In the United States it is estimated that over forty different styles emanating from Japan and Korea are being taught today – and this takes no account of the 200 or so Chinese-based styles very few of which are ever taught to non-Chinese. However, the objects of the majority of styles are in essence the same, despite the continuous factional strife which besets a great number of Japanese Karate schools. In keeping with the more traditional martial arts, Karate training in most schools is based on strict discipline. This of itself limits the number of students who will ever reach a high proficiency. The rigorous training soon alienates the majority of 'tyros' – the indolent, the dilettante, the undisciplined and those having no liking for competition and physical training will soon revert to the reverie in which they were probably entrenched before venturing into the world of martial arts.

In its advanced form, Karate combines physical energy with a psychological sophistication into what is considered by most experts of martial arts to be a formidable fighting machine. Whilst strength is the natural result of intensive training the startling exhibitions of penetrative power by experts are not the result of 'strength' in the normally accepted sense of the word. They are more the result of the correct application of widely accepted scientific facts.

PSYCHOLOGICAL PRINCIPLES OF KARATE

Due to the alleged connection between Karate and Buddhism and Zen, the underlying psychological principles have in the western world received much notice – in fact they probably receive more comment than they do in their home countries.

The basic psychological principles of Karate are stated to be concentration, calmness and confidence. The latter quality flows from a proficiency in the use of the two former principles. The Karate practitioner should strive to obtain a total awareness of the opponent's reactions, and he must also allow his own thoughts to flow freely and not consider his opponent's reaction in predetermined patterns.

Mokuso is the practicable method of practising meditation at the end of the day's training session. This is effected in the deep-seated position on the heels with the eyes shut. The mind should be cleared of all thoughts.

One further mental plus separates the student that succeeds from the one that does not – will-power.

The major psychological principles have been mentioned. The reverse of these mental pluses – agitation, lack of concentration, carelessness, and inflexibility – are the enemies of the Karateka. Training must help the student to develop mental control to enable him to meet the unexpected with equanimity.

THE PHYSICAL CHARACTERISTICS AND PRINCIPLES UNDERLYING KARATE TECHNIQUES

It is said that *Karate Technique* is the *Practice* of *Concentration* of *Strength* at the *Proper Time* and *Place*.

There are three main physical characteristics inherent in Karate. These are closely interrelated and are:

(a) speed of the blow, plus
(b) co-ordinated movement of body and extremity muscles, assisted by
(c) energy created by a reverse action.

As will be seen in the chapter dealing with breaking techniques, in Karate terms the *Power* of a blow depends upon the degree of efficient, i.e. concentrated, muscle power put into the blow plus the speed with which the blow is delivered. In physics terms:

Force = Mass × The Square of the *Velocity*

The serious student should consider these three most important physical characteristics and other physical principles in a little more detail.

Speed

Speed is the time required to deliver the striking force. It must be remembered that the striking *Power* of a force is inversely proportional to the time required for its application. Muscular strength by itself will not enable a student to reach the top in Karate. The effective use of that strength is the key and speed is one of the most important factors in the application of power.

Body Movement

The essential element is the transfer of power through the body to the target, utilising and combining the heavy strong and slow muscles of the body with the relatively fast extremity muscles *at the instant of impact*.

Obviously continual correct training over a period will make the transfer period progressively shorter.

Focus

The strength in the leg or arm alone is not sufficient. To obtain maximum power it is necessary to use all the parts of the body in co-ordination. Training is therefore conducted in such a way that all such available power is concentrated – i.e. *focused*, in the striking agent – hand, elbow, knee, foot, head, etc. – *at the instant of impact*. In order to achieve this focus, the tendons and muscles should be kept loose to allow the focus to be immediately responsive when needed.

It follows from this principle also that a knowledge of which muscles are used in a particular strike is very important.

Action and Reaction

A principle of physics is that every action has an opposite and equal reaction; practical examples in Karate technique are the rapid withdrawal of the non-striking arm, the lift of the jumping leg used as a springboard and the straightening and downward pressure of the rear leg into the ground adding power to the punch or strike.

One of the best examples of this physical principle is shown in the correct execution of the reverse thrust punch – *Gyakuzuki*. This strike is most effectively delivered in the forward leaning stance (*zenkutsu dachi*) with the striking arm opposite to the leading leg.

There are other physical principles which must be understood by students. The most important of these are:

Breath Control

This principle is of sufficient importance that a separate section of the

4

The punch begins with the power in the hips and stomach being transmitted through the abdominals, the chest, shoulders, arms and finally the fist.

All the body muscles are tensed at the moment of impact, and simultaneously the non-striking arm is snapped back to the ready punch position.

third chapter is devoted to it. The main point to be remembered is that inhaling relaxes the muscles – exhaling contracts them.

Timing

It may be considered rather obvious to state that if the timing of a strike is awry the blow will arrive too early or too late and will therefore be pointless. But as with most obvious principles, this is often forgotten unless brought to the student's attention.

Utilisation of Hip and Abdomen Power

The importance of the hip and abdomen in balance, in movement and in the co-ordination of muscles for a required movement, has long been emphasised in all Japanese martial arts. This area of the body linked to strong legs does produce the basic power and balance of the body. The gigantic shoulder arm and latissimus dorsi development of the 'Mr America'-type bodybuilder is not therefore encouraged in martial arts training, not because it is wrong, but simply because of itself it does not add anything to the student's ability and improvement in Karate.

KARATE-DO: THE SPIRITUAL CONSIDERATIONS

Karate is not merely a method of self-defence; its total concept lies far deeper than just physical cultivation. It is said that if physical development is the beginning of Karate, then mental development is the ultimate endeavour.

When we use the phrase *Karate-do*, we should emphasise *do* meaning 'the way', suggesting a higher degree of aspiration than learning just how to block, kick or punch.

The major purpose of Karate should be to train a person to achieve a level of perfection within his character by reaching a level of self-control. Such a person will have developed an awareness which may enable him to avoid or deflect situations of physical aggravation and potential violence which would, in a less developed person, require the application of his physical Karate abilities.

Mas Oyama Shihan's belief is that Karate should be non-violent – it ought to deny violence. One of Gichin Fimakoshi's precepts was 'there is no first attack in Karate'.

6

Perhaps this concept of the *way* of Karate may offer an explanation as to why large numbers of Americans and Europeans are joining classes (often expensive classes) to learn Karate. Perhaps it is the co-ordination of mental and physical development side by side which draws occidentals from their easy-going cultures, which have developed devastating methods of destruction, to an art of weaponless fighting which, even at its best, can never be a match for a gun and, at its worst, can be quite primitive.

Meditation

SHORT HISTORY OF KARATE

HISTORICAL ROOTS

With the interest in Japan and things Japanese which has flowered since the end of World War II, most Karate journalism and articles disseminated and issued to the public have given the impression that its origins are as Japanese as cherry blossom. Due to the not inconsiderable missionary zeal with which the Japanese have since 1950 set out to propagate the various Japanese Karate systems, it has been thought that Karate originated in Japan or at least in Okinawa. However, modern Karate teachers and students of Asian history consider it now established that the evidence points towards China as the place of origin. Hand-to-hand fighting with similar principles to modern Karate existed – and was being developed – in different parts of Asia before it was ever practised in Japan or the Ryukyu Islands.

Whilst basically as old as man himself, hand-to-hand fighting in its modern form, whether it is called Karate, Kung Fu, Kempo, Bersilat, etc., is of relatively recent origin.

In Japanese, the ideographs for Karate comprise two Chinese characters, *Kara* or in Chinese *T'ang* and *Te* or *Shou*. *Kara* denotes that it is of Chinese origin (the T'ang dynasty AD 618–960 being known as the Age of Enlightenment). *Te* means 'hands' or 'fist' – this term however was utilised to describe a style of fighting in Okinawa in the 17th century resembling modern Karate. Numerous other terms were and are used to describe the hand-to-hand systems. The principal terms were: *Kempo*, meaning 'way of the fist' (also read as *Ch'uan Fa* in Mandarin and *Ken Fat* in Cantonese), and *Gungfu* or *Kung Fu*, literally 'work master' or 'technique'.

The modern phrase 'empty hands' dates from the 1936 meeting of

8

the Okinawan masters sponsored by an Okinawan newspaper, at which the use of the *T'ang* character in the term *Karate* was discussed. The ideograph for *Kara* was altered to erase the Chinese connection for political reasons thus:

KARA
(T'ang)

TE
(Hand)

KARA
(Empty)

TE
(Hand)

Modern writers commenting on the origins of Karate seem in agreement that modern Karate did originate in China, and attention is drawn to the literature of the *Han* dynasty in which a book *Shou Pu* (a study on fist fighting – the first known book on this subject written in the pre-Christian era), indicates that Kempo was at that period relatively developed. Certainly, simultaneously with the development of the very numerous Chinese styles, similar fighting systems were developing in Egypt, India, Persia and most Asian countries, Thailand, Malaysia, Laos, Vietnam and Indonesia.

CHINA: THE CATALYST

Above all, however, China appears to have been the catalyst in developing and refining techniques now referred to as Karate.

Without a doubt bare-handed fighting was being developed in both India and China during the years before *Bodhidharma* first arrived in China in AD 520. No history of Karate – however concise – can be accurate without a short reference to Bodhidharma who has been called the 'original propagator of the martial arts concept'.* This Indian monk, who was the third child of a king and a brilliant student of Zen, was the legendary light in early Karate. Bodhidharma studied the attacking technique of animals and insects and the forces of nature, and, combining these with a special breathing technique, he created the basis for a legendary system of weaponless fighting and mental concentration. Bodhidharma created the Shaolin temple in Honan province and taught the monks there. The actual development of the Shaolin Ch'üan Fa system is very much open to doubt, but it is popularly held that the physical drills introduced by Bodhidharma† named *Shi Pa Lo Han Sho* – eighteen hands of the *Lo Han* – was the basis for the Shaolin Ch'üan Fa. The eighteen-point system, which was probably not intended for aggressive purposes, was subsequently revised to 170 techniques. From Bodhidharma's involvement it is suggested that Kung Fu was Buddhist-inspired, and for centuries Buddhist monks in China and Japan have studied Kempo, but mainly for physical exercise rather than for aggression.

THE BRIDGE THROUGH OKINAWA

How did Kung Fu thread its way from China to Japan? The link between the two great countries had, for several centuries, been through the Ryukyu Islands, for both the commercial and cultural aspects of life. It can be assumed that Ch'üan Fa was imported and grafted onto the natural fighting abilities of the Okinawans, and that the techniques, particularly of the Chinese military attachés, were no doubt carefully noted, copied and adapted. Okinawa itself had embassies in Thailand, Vietnam, Malaysia and other Asian states, and there was some immigration by Chinese settlers to Okinawa in the 14th century. The 'thirty families' (as they were called) are often credited with the introduction of Ch'üan Fa to the Ryukyu Islands. The Okinawan form was subsequently termed *Okinawa-te* (Okinawa hands).

* The Karate Dojo by Peter Urban.
* Karate: History and Tradition by Bruce A. Haines.

Probably the most significant date in the history of the development of modern Karate is the year 1609 when the Satsuma clan, led by the Shimazu family from Kyushu, having been beaten by the Tokugawa, mounted a military expedition against Okinawa and effectively gained control over the Ryukyus. This occupation in fact lasted until 1875, a period of over 250 years. A ban was ordered on all weapons, leaving any further resistance against the occupiers to be by weaponless methods.

The various resistance groups were forced to band together to form a united front and the different Ch'üan Fa and Tode styles were partially combined into a style simply referred to as *te* and which became known ultimately as *Okinawa-te*. Between 1630 and 1903, the art was practised in almost complete secrecy; the term *Karate* commenced to be used in the Ryukyus in the early 19th century, but even today in Okinawa it is not universally accepted as the correct term to describe the art.

After 1903, Karate tended to be classified into the various *Ryu* which developed from the rival schools based at Naha, Shuri and Tomari.

JAPAN: KARATE, THE ECLECTIC SYSTEM

There were numerous highly-developed forms of unarmed combat known and practised in Japan well before the 20th century. Certainly the monks who studied Buddhism in China learnt Ch'üan Fa even as far back as the 7th century, but most of the recorded instruction of the Japanese in punching and striking technique was learnt from visiting Chinese artisans, or gleaned from forages by the Japanese military forces into Korea. The Japanese had many and varied forms – Bujutsu Yawara, Jiu Jitsu, Torite and Kenjutsu, to name but the most widely known. Professor Kano, however, always maintained that the Ch'üan Fa techniques differed so radically from Jiu Jitsu that there was no possibility of connection between them. A study of Jiu Jitsu shows that blows were struck, not with the clenched fist, but with the inner or little-finger edge of the palm. Fingertip jabs seem also to have been much practised and utilised. The nearest techniques to Karate strikes which were practised in Japan prior to the Okinawan masters coming to Japan after 1910 were the Atemi Waza (strikes to the vital parts of the body), which were an important part of the Jiu Jitsu technique and are still part of the total Judo art although not usually taught to students.

11

The individual who made the greatest impact on Japanese Budo men and has been called the father of modern Karate is Gichin Funakoshi, a physically small (5′ 1″) Okinawan who demonstrated his art at the Butokuden in Kyoto in 1915. The Japanese Budo men were much impressed by Funakoshi's abilities and he was prevailed upon to stay in Japan from May 1922 until he died there at the age of eighty-six in 1957. Funakoshi, a frail youth, began his study of Karate under Itosu when he was thirteen, and later studied under Matsumura. It is believed that he studied most of the main styles: Nahate, Goju Ryu, Uechi Ryu and Shito Ryu. Funakoshi was already well into middle-age, in fact fifty-one years old, when he took up full-time Karate teaching in Japan and for several years he had to supplement his earnings by utilising his ability at calligraphy. Between 1924 and 1931 he took under his wing several university and high school clubs which became the foundation, together with his main dojo at Meijuro (Tokyo), of the Shotokan School, which is now in the Suidobashi district of Tokyo.

Funakoshi consistently stressed the philosophical side of his art and this contributed very much to the difficulty which he encountered in building up his schools in Japan. The main part of his teaching was Kata combined with exercises and etiquette. Free fighting seemed to form little part of his teaching – certainly until the Katas had been mastered – and this resulted in many Karate students leaving the style, the most famous of these being Mas Oyama, the founder of Kyo-kushinkai and Otsuka who left to found Wado Ryu. Also during the 1930s other Okinawan styles had opened schools in Japan, notably Goju Ryu under Chojun Miyagi, Kempo under Muneiomi Sawayama and Shito Ryu under Kenwas Manbuni. After a defeat by the Goju school, the Funakoshi school began teaching and emphasising much more the importance of Jiyu Kumite (free fighting).

Funakoshi's main contributions to the development of modern Karate in Japan were the systemizing of Karate technique and Kata, and the instilling into students of the ethics of discipline found in most other martial arts. The precepts he preached, 'Karate begins and ends with courtesy' and 'There are no offensive techniques in Karate' (which later is found on the monument to this famous teacher in the Engakuji Zen temple at Kita Kamakura) do more to sum up Funakoshi's attitude to Karate and life than any short article can possibly serve to do.

CALISTHENICS
and BODY TRAINING

CORRECT BREATHING

The breathing exercises are one of the most essential phases of Karate training. The intention is not only to refresh the respiratory system, but also to strengthen the lower abdomen area. Consequently the Karate breathing exercises are abdominal exercises.

The importance of correct breathing is due to the vital rule of mastering body tension and the concentration of strength at a given second, both of which can only be obtained to a high degree by correct breathing technique.

It is a principle of physics that the greatest force will be developed by the body at the point when one half of the lungs' air capacity has been expelled. Weightlifters and most other sportsmen in the 'iron game' of field events, shot-put, javelin and discus are very aware of this. In Karate the use of the *Kiai* or shout is one example of the use of breath control.

To examine the principles of Karate breathing further it is necessary to consider the three main divisions:

(a) Normal breathing
(b) Ibuki
(c) Nogare

Normal breathing is the usual quiet everyday breathing using the chest. All forms of breathing have two sides, the 'input' and 'output'. When a person is exhilarated or laughing, the emphasis is on the output; if the person is scared, the emphasis will be on input. Breath control is necessary to restore normal breathing after exertion.

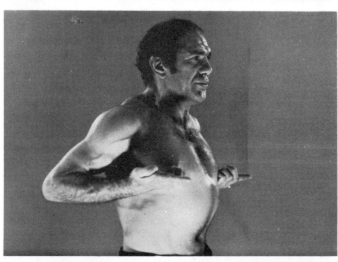

NOGARE

This method of breathing is used in actual combat or practice fighting to maintain composure and control. The breath should be inhaled deeply and quietly through the nose, held for a few seconds and then exhaled through the mouth in a controlled manner. The tongue is placed behind the teeth to silence the sound of the breathing.

Practise of this particular breathing technique will help in the development of the diaphragm which is all-important in Karate training. (See page 14–16).

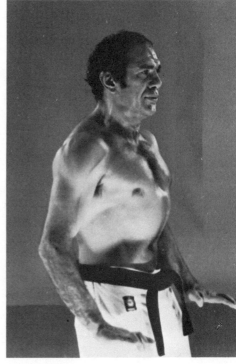

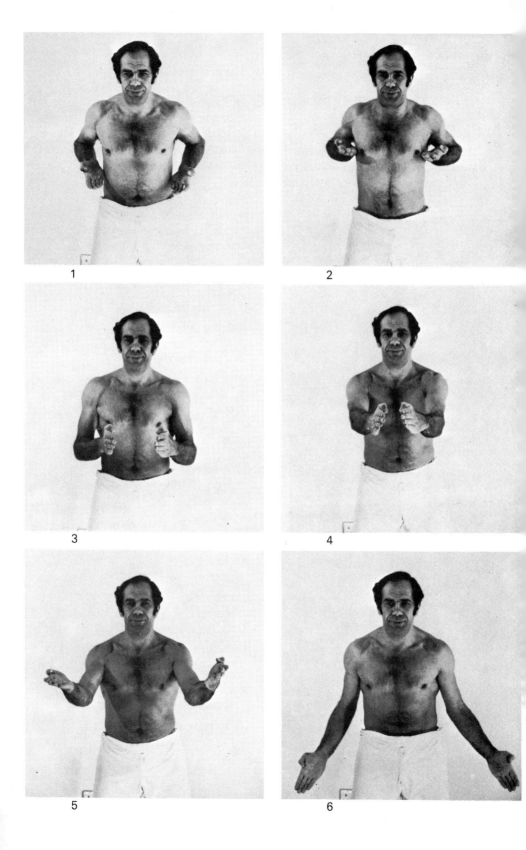

1

2

3

4

5

6

Breathe in through to diaphragm

Open mouth wide

IBUKI

Ibuki is involved in both the Sanchin and Tensho Katas which are dealt with in detail later on in the eighth chapter.

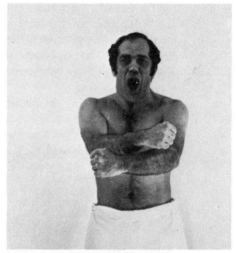

Tense stomach and force breath out from stomach

When you feel breath has been expelled, tense abdomen and try to expel out more breath

Ibuki can be used to restore normal breathing after a strong blow to the diaphragm or stomach which has left one weak or winded.

THE IMPORTANCE OF KIAI

The use of Kiai has already been mentioned. In short, Kiai is a piercing yell or shout generated from the lower abdomen and can be compared to the roar of a tiger when jumping towards its prey. It will increase the confidence of the person effecting the technique and will, if effected correctly, tend to lessen the opponent's confidence and, if unsuspecting, the opponent may also be startled. It also enables the attacker's mind to be cleared and to commit himself totally to his technique.

Such is the physical manifestation of Kiai that it is claimed that masters can use the Kiai to stun a person at a distance!

GENERAL BODY TRAINING

Every training session should *commence* and *end* with exercises. At the beginning of the session you need to loosen and tone the muscles, joints and tendons, and at the end of the session you need to relax the body and guard against stiffness.

Karate exercises are aimed particularly at strengthening and stretching the joints and tendons, rather than the muscles of the body. It is usual to start at the toes and work upwards. All the following parts of the body should be covered; the joints, ankles, knees, hips, vertebrae, wrists, fingers, elbows and neck.

20

Notice the difference between the position of
fingers above and below

The above exercises are aimed specifically at the needs of the Kara-teka. It is each individual's responsibility to maintain his own good health by daily training, diet and proper regular exercising.

Obviously, for most people, an increase in bodily strength and body condition is necessary to obtain a high standard in Karate in addition to that which will be obtained by the calisthenic exercises and standard Karate training. The correct use of weights and barbells can increase the rate of growth of bodily strength and should be considered by all serious students. However, the proportion of weight training to general Karate training should be kept under control. Serious students, who do four days per week of Karate training, should spend not more than two additional days on weight training.

Other types of exercises particularly useful to students are skipping, running (particularly sprinting), most forms of jumping and leaping, swimming, fencing, ballet and gymnastics.

STANCES and POSITIONS

GENERAL EXPLANATION

The stances or positions in Karate differ from those used in normal everyday living. Karate stances are designed to facilitate the requirements of certain techniques.

It is true to say that many of the classic Karate stances are not very suitable for free fighting or combat. This is because many of the stances used in training are designed particularly for building up strength in the legs and lower part of the body, and for obtaining good balance and movement, rather than for swift movement. Balance is the most important point of any stance.

In all stances, whether the legs are bent or not, the upper portion of the body or trunk must be perpendicular. If this is not maintained, the performance of a technique with power will not be possible. Although perpendicular, the body can still be turned to present the smallest target area to the opponent.

Due to the lack of leg development by Westerners, most of the stances and the movements in the stances are found to be unnatural and therefore require a considerable degree of practice.

As mentioned before, most classic stances are not suitable for combat or sparring (Kumite). For fighting purposes the strongest stances, i.e. those with the best basic balance and permitting rapid movement in any direction, are used. Even then, the strongest stances will normally be shortened for quicker mobility. Stances which are particularly suitable for sparring are described in the chapter on Free Fighting.

DETAILED EXPLANATION OF MAIN STANCES

The stances shown in the next few pages must be mastered by all serious students.

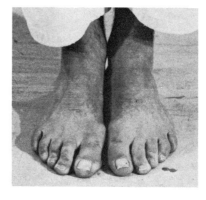

right: Normal Stance (Heisoku Dachi)
The body is held upright in this stance and in Musubi Dachi, Heiko Dachi, Uchi Hachiji Dachi and Fudo Dachi stances.

In these stances the legs are tensed and the torque in the legs is to the centre point between the knees. The backside is tensed and the whole body is tightened and not allowed to sag.

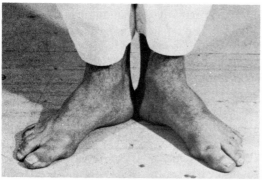

Open Toe Stance (Musubi Dachi)
The heels are together

Parallel Stance (Heiko Dachi)

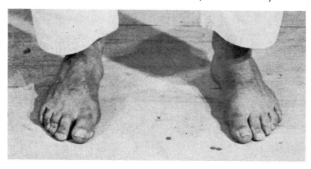

Pigeon Toe Stance (Uchi Hachiji Dachi)
Feet are approximately a shoulder-width apart in both these stances

Stable or Ready Stance (Fudo Dachi)
The comments on the normal stance about tensing the body and the torque in the legs apply also to this stance.
The width of the legs is shoulder wide and the feet point slightly outwards. This stance is used principally when standing waiting for instructions or when resting between techniques.

Sumo Stance (Shiko Dachi)
The feet are at an angle of approximately 45° and pull towards the rear. The width of the feet is 1½ to 2 shoulders.

below left and right:
Straddle Stance (Kiba Dachi)
Again 1½ to 2 shoulders wide. The knees should press out until they are almost over the feet. The feet try to push inwards together. The feet are parallel.

Forward Leaning Stance
(Zenkutsu Dachi)
The feet are shoulder wide, and the rear foot is approximately two shoulders back.
The knee of the front leg is over the ball of the foot, and the back leg is tensed until the knee will not bend when pressure is put on it suddenly. About 60% of the body weight is on the front leg.

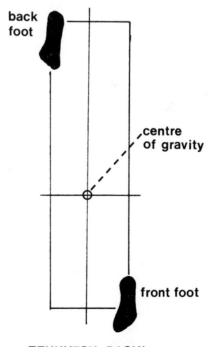

back foot

centre of gravity

front foot

ZENKUTSU DACHI

Back Leaning Stance
(Kokutsu Dachi)
The weight distribution is about 70% on the rear leg and about 30% on the front leg.
One foot steps forward about three foot lengths and the heel is raised. The rear leg is bent at the knee. The front leg is in a line about 1 to 2 inches to the side of the heel of the rear foot.

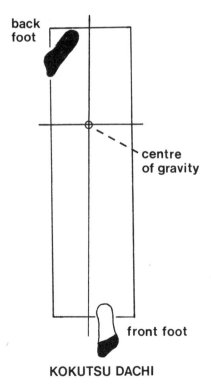

KOKUTSU DACHI

Sanchin Stance (Sanchin Dachi)
This is sometimes described as the Hour-glass Stance. The feet are about shoulder wide or fractionally wider. Both feet have the toes pointed in at a 45° angle.
The heel of the front foot is in a line with the toes of the rear foot.
The legs bend at the knees along the line of the feet.
The whole body is highly tensed and the trunk is straight.
This is one of the best stances for developing a strong diaphragm, and for building all round strength. Hence much of the basic techniques are practised in this stance.
The weight is spread evenly on each leg.

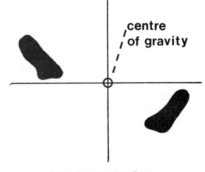

centre
of gravity

SANCHIN DACHI

37

Cat Stance (Neko Ashi Dachi)
This is similar to the back leaning stance, but the stance is much shorter. The front foot is not so far forward and the weight distribution is now approximately 90% on the rear foot and only 10% on the front foot.

This stance and the Back Leaning Stance (Kokutsu Dachi) are considered in detail in the chapter on Free Fighting.

Crane Stance (Tsuru Ashi Dachi)

Hooked Stance (Kake Dachi)

MOVEMENT

Movement may be by sliding, stepping, jumping or turning. It can be said as a general principle, however, that steps as in everyday walking are not used. It is better to slide the feet forward, or back, rather than to lift them. The following main rules cover the guidelines for movement in Karate stance:

(a) The whole body moves as one, but the hip – or rather the centre of gravity – controls the balance.
(b) The trunk remains perpendicular even when the legs are bent.
(c) The head remains at the same height if the body is being shifted in a particular stance.
(d) The feet slide along the surface of the ground but not in such a way as to slow the speed of the advance or retreat. The weight of the body must move smoothly and always under control.

It goes without saying that the better the form of the stance is maintained in movement, the better will be the balance.

ATTACKING TECHNIQUES

Any part of the body which can move can be utilised in attack. There are therefore three principal body parts utilised in attacking technique: the arm(s), the leg(s) and the head.

The basic striking weapon in Karate is the fist – referred to as the 'soul'. Special attention should always be given to the correct forming of the fist and the 'tempering' of this weapon above all others, including regular practice with the *makiwara* (padded board).

Whilst this chapter is not in any way intended to be exhaustive on the subject of classification of techniques, it includes the majority of striking techniques which are most commonly found and utilised.

TECHNIQUE CLASSIFICATION

Hand Technique (Tewaza)

(i) Forefist (Seiken)

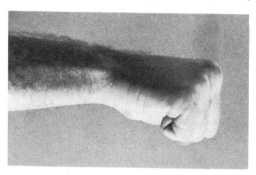

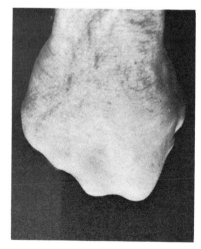

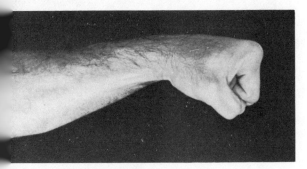

(i) Forefist (Seiken)

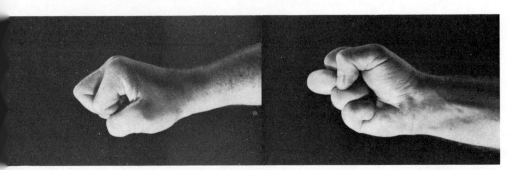

(ii) One Knuckle Fist (Nakayubi Ipponken)

(iii) Thumb Knuckle Fist (Oyayubi Ipponken)

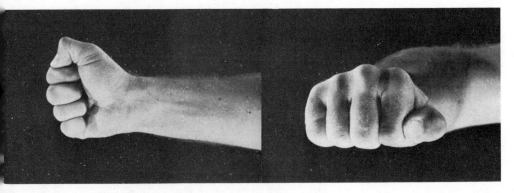

(iv) Dragon's Head Fist (Ryutoken) (This is between Hiraken and Seiken)

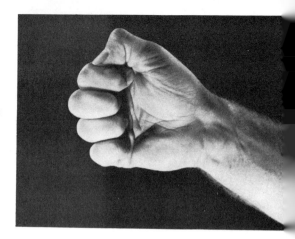

(v) Flat or Level Fist (Hiraken)

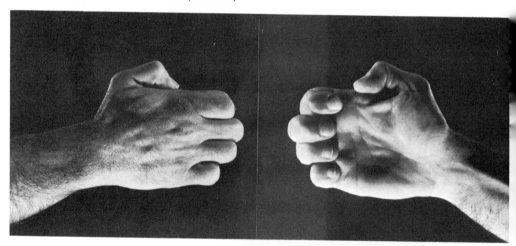

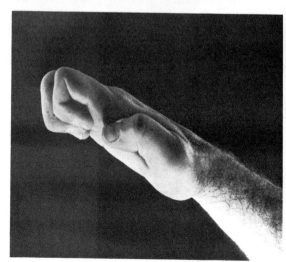

(vi) Inverted Fist (Uraken)

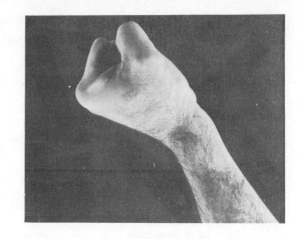

(vii) Spear Head (Yohon Nukite)

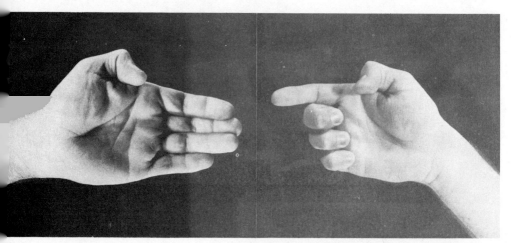

Nukite can be done with the fingers tightly together (as above right) or with some fingers only, i.e. one finger (Ippon Nukite), two fingers (Nihon Nukite, right). The latter technique is generally used against the eyes only.

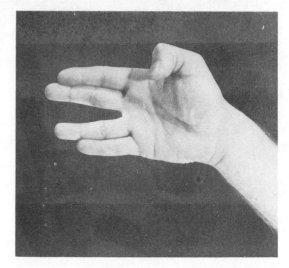

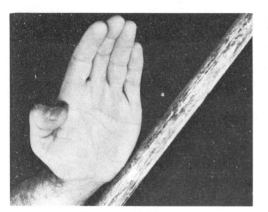

(viii) Knife Hand
(Shuto or Tegatana)

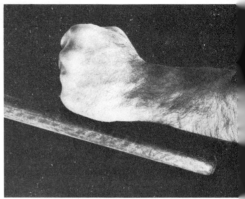

(ix) Hammer Fist (Tettsui or Kentsui)

(x) Flat Hand (Haishu or Hirate)

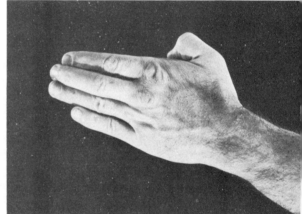

(xi) Inner Knife Hand (Haito)

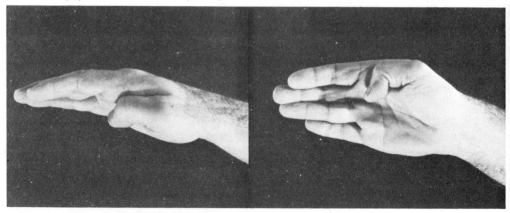

44

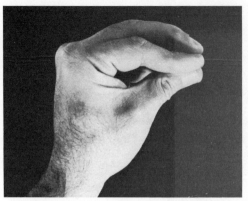

(xii) Chicken Beak Hand (Keiko)

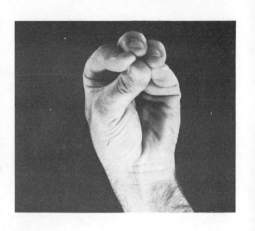

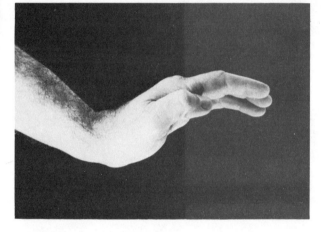

(xiii) Palm Heel (Shotei)

(xiv) Wrist (Koken)

(xv) Elbow (Empi or Hiji)

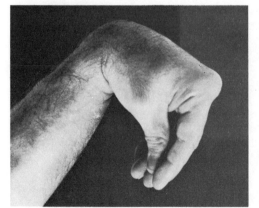

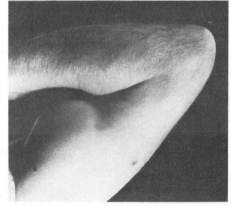

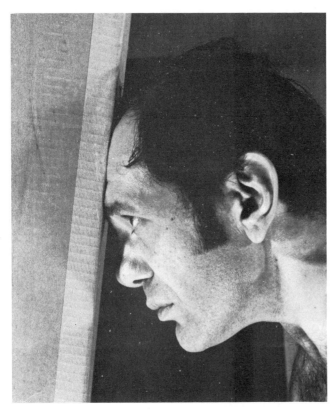

(xvi) Head (Atama)

Foot and Leg Technique (Ashiwaza)

(i) Ball of Foot (Chusoku)

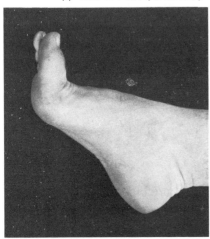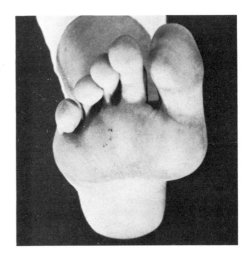

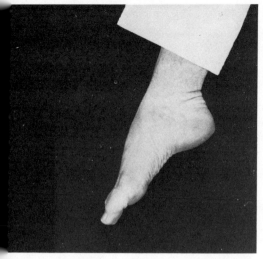
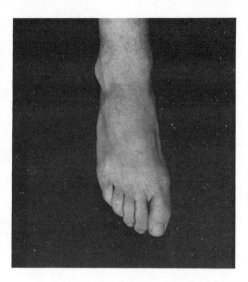

(ii) Instep (Haisoku)

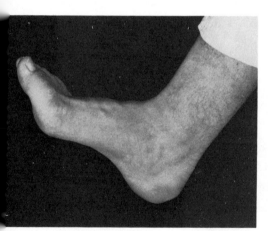

(iii) Heel (Kakato)

(v) Knee (Hiza)

(iv) Knife Foot (Sokuto or Ashigatana)

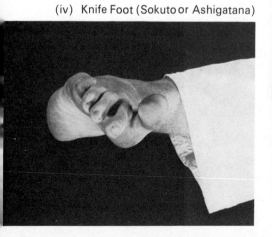

METHODS OF STRIKING (Zukiwaza and Uchiwaza)

The forefist (Seiken) is the most important striking surface in Japanese-style Karate. Very great care must be taken to ensure that the fist is correctly formed. An incorrectly formed fist, particularly a loose fist, will suffer substantial damage if a blow is actually struck against the makiwara (punching board) or against an attacker in the street.

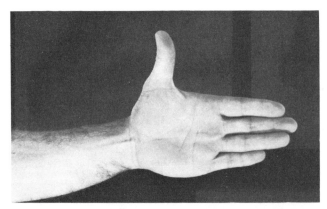

How to make a forefist:

(1)

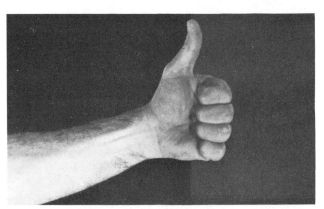

(2)

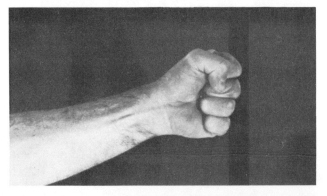

(3)

Points to consider when striking with Thrust Punch (Seiken Tsuki):

(a) The forearm and knuckles must form a straight line.
(b) The power must be concentrated straight through without bending the wrist.
(c) The strike follows a straight line from the nipple position and the arm must brush the body.
(d) The wrist (and fist) turns to engage momentarily before contact.
(e) The shoulders do not go forward – power comes from the hips and latissimus dorsi muscles not the shoulders.

Lining up punch to centre-line.

'Kamaite' – ready to punch.

Seiken Chudan Tsuki

Seiken Jodan Tsuki

Seiken Gedan Tsuki

Uraken Mawashi Uchi

Uraken Shomen Uchi

Uraken Yoko Ganmen

Uraken Hizo Uchi

Shita Tsuki

Shuto Yoko Ganmen Uchi

Shuto Sakotsu Uchi

Hiji Jodan Ate

Hiji Chudan Ate

Hiji Age

Hiji Ago

Oroshi

Tate Tsuki Chudan

Tate Tsuki Jodan

Koken Uchi Jodan

Haito Uchi Jodan

Hiraken Chudan

Hiraken Jodan

Tettsui Oroshi
Ganmen Uchi

Hiraken Oroshi
(Diagonal cut across
face)

METHODS OF KICKING (KERI WAZA)

Points to be borne in mind:

(a) Generally, the knee is raised towards the chest, or, if the kick is to
the side, as high as the knee can be drawn up at the side of the body –
so that the thigh is horizontal with the ground. The higher the height of
the target the higher the height over the horizontal that the knee should
be raised. An added bonus of lifting the knee to aid the kick is that the

57

raised knee and shin can be utilised in blocking (see sixth chapter).

(b) The supporting (non-kicking) leg must be firmly planted on the ground with the knee slightly bent.

(c) The foot of the supporting leg remains flat on the ground.

(d) The kicking foot is retracted as swiftly as possible following the kick to prevent the opponent seizing this.

(e) The hips are normally thrust behind the kick.

(f) The hands and arms must be controlled and not allowed to flap.

(g) The body and head lean into the kick rather than away.

Mae Keage: Note position of supporting feet and hands.

Mae Geri – front kick to waist with ball of foot
From side

From front

Hiza Geri

Hiza Ganmen Geri

Kick against opponent

From side

Mawashi Geri — with ball of foot

From front

Strike — note supporting leg turned to 90° for support combined with hip swinging in to give power.

Steps in Mawashi Geri Leg raised horizontally to the side

Against opponent's head

Foot and leg return to the
first position, and thence . . .

. . . to the ground.

Mawashi Kubi Geri is similar but the strike is with the instep (Haisoku) against the neck.

below and above opposite: Yoko Geri (Sokuto) — thrust side kick

From the side

From the front

Jodan Yoko Geri against opponent

Kansetsu Geri (Fumikomi) and Kakato Geri.

Against fallen opponent

Ushiro Geri
From the side

Against opponent – Chu

In Kansetsu Geri, the knife foot is used against the opponent's knee, from the side or behind. In Kakato Geri, either to the front or rear, the heel is the striking surface. In any of these 'stamping' kicks the knee is drawn towards the chest – and returns to this position before being replaced on the ground.

Against opponent – Jodan

The kick can be swung diagonally to the opponent (often called 'wheel kicks') or directly to the rear. Note the position of the head.

Chudan   Jodan
Mae Tobi Geri

JUMPING KICKS

Mawashi Tobi Geri

below and right: Ushiro Tobi Geri
Chudan

Yoko Tobi Geri

Jodan

Jumping Ushiro Mawashi Geri

BASIC TRAINING

Training on individual techniques will take place by repetition either in a static position or in consecutive movement forward and back. Initially, students will practice basic strikes, punches, blocks and kicks in Heiko Dachi (the Parallel Stance) and after the techniques are understood by the students and some degree of technical correctness is attained, the stances of Sanchin Dachi (Hour-Glass Stance) and Kiba Dachi (Horse Stance) will be used.

At the stage of the introduction of Sanchin Dachi, movement forward and back is also introduced to the student. The stance firstly and primarily employed is the Forward Leaning Stance (Zenkutsu Dachi) and in this stance all techniques of striking, blocking and kicking will be practised in movement.

The Back Leaning Stance (Kokutsu Dachi) and other stances will be used in movement including Sanchin Dachi, Kiba Dachi, and Neko Ashi Dachi (Cat Stance).

In forward, turning and backward movements, the basic techniques will be practised until a considerable degree of technical correctness is obtained. Then, progressively, a combination of techniques, blocks and punches, blocks and kicks will be phased into the training, together with the simple Katas. The number of combinations which can be practised is legion.

BLOCKING TECHNIQUES

CLASSIFICATION OF HAND BLOCKS

(a) With closed fist (Seiken)

(b) With (open) knife hand (Shuto)

(c) Palm Heel (Shotei)

(d) Wrist (Koken)

(e) Lower Forearm (Kote)

CLASSIFICATION OF LEG BLOCKS

(a) Thigh Block (Kaji Uke)

(b) Knee Block (Hiza Uke)

(c) Shin Block (Sune Uke)

(d) Instep Block (Heisoku Uke)

(e) Foot (arch) Block (Teisoku Uke)

MAIN PRINCIPLES OF KARATE BLOCKING

(a) The intention is to deflect the blow; the body trunk will turn to present a smaller target area.

(b) The best *carried out* blocks will, when completed, leave the attacker open and the blocker in a position to retaliate immediately.

(c) Right-angle blocks against the striking arm are less effective than
   (i) circular blocks which describe an arc, e.g. Chudan Uchi Uke, Chudan Soto Uke,
   (ii) inclined blocks, e.g. Jodan Uke.

It follows from this that the smaller the angle formed by the blocking arm with the attacking arm the less shock will be felt by the blocker and less force will be required to divert the direction of the attack. The mawashi or circular blocks are of Chinese origin though often now adopted by Japanese styles.

(d) The blocks should be effected in such a way as to provide a shock

69

value, in order to produce a demoralising effect on the attacker, to obviate the necessity for a retaliatory attack.

Equally as important as the pure blocking techniques are the dodging or avoidance techniques, whether these comprise merely moving or swaying the head and upper body or shifting the entire body including the legs and feet. Examples of techniques which should be practised are given after the next section on methods of blocking.

METHOD OF BLOCKING

1 Hand and Arm Blocks

Jodan Uke (upper block)

Completed movement with opponent

Chudan Soto Uke (middle outer block)

Chudan Uchi Uke (middle inner block)

Completed movement with opponent

Completed movement with opponent

Gedan Barai (lower parry)

Juji Uke (cross block)
Note: the left leg is
forward and the left
hand under the
block

Shuto Jodan Uke

Shotei Chudan Uke

Shuto Uchi Uke Jodan

75

| Shuto Chudan Soto Uke | Shotei Jodan Uke | Shotei Gedan Uke |

Block and Retaliation

As previously mentioned in the section on Main Principles earlier in this chapter, if a block is correctly executed and the person blocking remains on balance, not only will the attacker's blow be deflected but the attacker will be open to a retaliatory strike if effected swiftly. These are some simple examples when practised as an attack followed by a parry defence and retaliation; this is known as one step sparring (Ippon Kumite).

| Haito Uchi Uke | Koken Jodan Uke | Morote Uke |

It is assumed for demonstration purposes that the attacker will commence the attack in Zenkutsu Dachi as in the photograph below.

Jodan Tsuki attack
blocked with
Seiken Jodan Uke. →

Chudan Tsuki
attack, block
Chudan Soto Uke. →

Jodan Tsuki
attack, parry with
Jodan Uke. →

Retaliate with Hiji
→ Jodan Ate.

Step to side and
→ retaliate with Jodan
Tsuki to side of
head.

Retaliate with Hiza
→ Mawashi Geri
Chudan.

Further examples are demonstrated in the chapter on Karate Sparring and Free Fighting.

2 Foot and Leg Blocks

These are normally fairly advanced techniques and require the defender to maintain a good balanced position. The advantage of leg or foot blocks is that they leave both hands free for immediate retaliation.

Teisoku Mawashi Uke (roundhouse foot block)

Sune Uke (shin block)

Having effected any of these leg blocks the same leg can be immediately utilised again for attack with a kicking technique.

ADVANCED BLOCKING TECHNIQUES

Having considered pure blocking techniques, it is now necessary to look at techniques for avoiding the attacking blow altogether.

As already emphasised, a well executed block will immediately leave the blocker in a position to retaliate. In practice, one rarely sees a block correctly executed in a Karate competition or in club practice fighting; furthermore, in the authors' view it is virtually impossible to effectively block a Western boxer's fast punches with basic Karate blocking techniques. Most basic Karate blocking technique – whether from Japanese or Chinese schools – is a holding technique, and, unless he has been blocked by the defender, the attacker is not prevented from continuing his attack.

Whilst basic techniques must be mastered before more advanced techniques are attempted, advanced Karate technique indicates the following methods of dealing with attacks as being the most effective:
(a) Simultaneous deflection and counter-attack.
(b) 'Dodging' the attack in such a way as to immediately facilitate a retaliation.
(c) Simultaneous strike.

Wing Chun (Chinese boxing), a modern style of Kung Fu which is now popular in Hong Kong and which emphasises the practical side of Kung Fu technique, particularly draws attention to the deflection and simultaneous retaliation method, on the basis that this enables the retaliatory blow to be struck with the first movement by the defender instead of the second or the third.

Simultaneous Deflection and Counter-attack

This will normally be effected by one arm or leg, blocking or deflecting; the other arm or leg is used to retaliate.

In expert form, any movement made by the defender towards the attacker, the block itself and the retaliation are performed as a continuous move.

In both the simultaneous deflection and counter-attack techniques and the simultaneous strike techniques, it will be found advantageous to keep the arms in a forward position, elbows low; this facilitates easier deflections as the hands will be usually inside the attacking arm or leg.

Dodging and Avoiding Techniques

In simple terms, this means shifting the body out of the path of attack:

ducking, weaving, rotating or any other method of avoiding the blow whilst leaving the defender on balance. The most effective method often is to move rapidly towards the attacker rather than away from him.

None of these advanced methods will be effective unless the defender moves with considerable speed and has reached a stage in his Karate

Open left
hand block

Right hand
retaliation
(Jodan Tsuki)

development at which he has some ability to anticipate his attacker's movements.

The concept of moving against the opponent with simultaneous blows being delivered against the attacker will normally surprise and may unbalance the opponent leaving the initiative with the person originally attacked. This is particularly so against Mawashi Geri or Yoko Geri.

Ducking below the strike

Turn body inside blow and strike with open hand

Shift body outside attacking arm; having moved whole body to side of blow, retaliate with Jodan Tsuki.

Similar Technique Used Against Kicks

Against Mae Geri – simple dodge tactic

Against Mawashi Geri – hook the standing leg away

Against Kanzetsu Geri

Simultaneous Strike

This is the most effective strike to carry out and the most devastating to receive. It is also the most dangerous and difficult to effect and requires the exponent to have considerable confidence in his abilities as well as split-second timing.

The simplest form of this attack/defence is to punch faster than the attacker and thereby hit the target – the attacker – first. As indicated in the section earlier on simultaneous deflection and counter-attack, the deflection punch can be delivered quickest from the middle body position or alternatively by the arm closest to the attacker's arm. In this technique, the precept 'attack is the best form of defence' is seen to advantage.

Anticipate and attack first.

Deflection punch over opponent's strike. Note: shoulders turned.

Deflection punch under opponent's strike. Note: shoulders turned.

Similar Attack Defences Against Kick Attacks

Against Mawashi, attack groin with two hands.

Against Mawashi, hook leg away with back reaping movements.

KARATE FORMS—KATA

BACKGROUND AND PURPOSE

In the Kata, a number of pre-determined defences and attacks are performed in a fixed order of succession. All styles of Karate, whether of Chinese, Japanese, Korean or Okinawan origin, include Kata as part of the total training. Some styles include as many as fifty Katas (Shotokan), some about fifteen (Kyokushinkai and Goju): Wing Chun (Chinese boxing) has only three.

Many of the Katas taught today are of very old origin, having been varied and modified from time to time by masters who had their own interpretations of the movements. Even today, the masters of a style will change a technique, stance or movement after many years of long practice and meditation on a particular Kata.

In Karate, unlike Judo, few techniques can be demonstrated to their logical conclusion without the likelihood of injuring the sparring partner; therefore the method of focusing the blow a split-second before striking has been developed for sparring practice. Because of this great emphasis in Karate training is placed on the study of the forms. Some are simple and short, others long and more complicated. Some Katas are designed to show speed, some to emphasise and practise special methods of breathing, and some are designed to stress dynamic tension.

Kata represents the art in Karate-do, without which Karate would be only an efficient method of combat. In Kata the student has to attain flexibility of technique and stance. In Kumite (sparring) the student will tend to use and rely upon his favourite and strongest techniques and stances, since the emphasis is on winning or, often, on not losing. In sparring, therefore, he will be loath to attempt positions

87

and techniques in which he has less than full confidence – in Kata he will have to employ a multitude of different stances and techniques, and attain a degree of proficiency in all of them.

The main purposes of practising Kata can be summarised as follows:

(a) To link basic practice and free fighting.
(b) To practise a wide number of different techniques in different directions and situations, usually in movement.
(c) To obtain rhythm and continuity of technique.
(d) To obtain *technical perfection* and a fusion of speed, balance, strength and timing.

A Kata is initially practised slowly without power to ensure technical accuracy and textbook stances. When complete accuracy of technique and balance is achieved, the degree of power in each technique is increased progressively and, simultaneously, the total time taken for the execution of each technique (and the total Kata) is reduced.

A view often put forward is that Kata is intended to be a practice for suggested defence and attack techniques by a number of imaginary opponents. The authors' view is that this is an incorrect conception. The execution of each technique has to be performed with such exactly correct form and textbook style, that such techniques would rarely be viable and effective in street fighting.

Many of the most important Katas taught in the Kyokushinkai and Goju-Kai styles were derived from the original Chinese Kempo techniques and are based on the movements of animals. The most famous Kata devised by Gichin Funakoshi, the euphemistically styled Dai Nippon Karate-do Ten No Kata (literally, Great Japan Karate Way Heavenly Kata), is comprised of ten movements only.

The main two groups of Kata taught by the Japanese-based schools are the three Taikyoku Katas – Taikyoken Shodan, Nidan, Sandan (Essential Karate Kata First, Second, Third Step) – and the five Pinan (or Heian) Katas (First Step to Fifth Step).

The Katas shown in this book are Taikyoku I, Sanchin and Saifa.

Sanchin and Tensho

The Sanchin and Tensho Katas are vital basic forms, particularly because they require a study of the special Karate breathing method,

Ibuki, which was described in the third chapter.

In both Katas, the Sanchin (Hour-Glass) Stance is employed throughout and one of the objects is to attain greater bodily strength, particularly a powerful diaphragm, by the use of dynamic tension movements. The Sanchin Kata emphasises the middle thrust punch. The Tensho Kata practises predominantly open hand blocking techniques – *Ten* suggests rotation, and *Sho* means 'hand'. Chojun Miyagi, the founder of Goju Ryu, suggests that Sanchin indicates power, stiffness and strength; Tensho, on the other hand, implies softness.

The Tensho Kata shows the Tensho blocking techniques, i.e. palm, heel blocks, open hand blocks and wrist techniques, the intention being to enable the blocking hand to remain in contact with the attacking agent. Similar wrist rolling techniques are shown in the first Wing Chun Kata, *Siu Lim Tao*.

In Sanchin Kata the movements are effected slowly and with great power. The time employed on most movements is five seconds, except on the two 180° turns about one third of the way through the Kata, and on the two movements back simultaneously with the Mawashi Uke (Roundhouse Block) at the end, which four moves are effected quickly.

The following series of photographs shows the movements in Sanchin Kata.

1 Musubi Dachi. Eyes closed.   2 Eyes open.

5   6

3 Throw hands up, rise onto balls of feet. Take in quick breath.

4–7 Pull hands down, closing fists and complete Ibuki breathing.

7

8–10 Step forward with right leg . . .

. . . in half circle into Sanchin stance; effect double arm block.

. . . Ibuki breathing.

14–15 Breathe in quickly, then block with left hand and effect . . .

11 Breath in quickly and quietly;
pull left arm back slowly.

. . . Ibuki breathing.

12–13 Punch left arm slowly . . .
16 Breathe quickly, move forward
left leg in half circle into Sanchin
stance, then pull back right arm.

17–19 Repeat same movements and breathing technique as in 12–15 . . .

21–22 Punch under right elbow and Ibuki.

. . . but with right arm.

20 Right leg forward into Sanchin stance, left hand back slowly.

23–24 Turn body to left, step forward right foot.

25–26 Complete 180° turn with quick movement, effect left arm inside block.

29–30 Pull back left hand, Ibuki, and punch under right elbow.

27–28 Slow punch right arm, Ibuki breathing, block with right arm.

31–34 Exactly similar movements as 21–24.

33

34

37

38 Step forward with right foot.

35–37 Exactly similar movements as in 16–19.

39–41 Similar movements as in 13–15.

Without taking any further step the punch and breaking out movement is performed by the right hand and again by the left hand.

41

44   45

42–45 Throw hands forward, palms out, breathe in and pull hands back fast.

46–48 With Ibuki, push hands forward into spear hand.

48

The hooking and pull back movement, and the push out with both hands are performed twice more.

49–57 Step back with right foot still in Sanchin stance and effect Roundhouse block. Ibuki from 55–57.

53   54

55   56

. . . Sanchin stance and effect Roundhouse block. Ibuki from 64–66.

57

58–66 Step back with left foot still in . . .

61

62

63

64

66

67 Move right foot back in Musubi Dachi.

65

68 Eyes closed.

Taikyoku I, II and III

Originally compiled by Gichin Funakoshi, these three forms are simple as regards both the technique to be executed and the pattern (footwork) which makes up the different stances of these Katas.

In Taikyoku I and II, the stance used throughout is the Forward Leaning Stance (Zenkutsu Dachi). The techniques used are middle thrust punch (Seiken Chudan Tsuki) and lower block (Mae Gedan

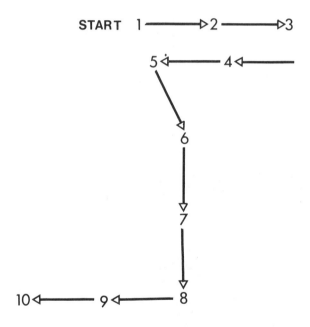

Barai) in Taikyoku I, and the variation in Taikyoku II is to change the punch to the upper thrust punch (Seiken Jodan Tsuki).

In Taikyoku III, both punches are used and also the middle inner block (Seiken Chudan Uchi Uke), and a further stance on the turning movements only – the Back Leaning Stance (Kokutsu Dachi).

The pattern of the three Taikyokus is roughly that of an 'H'.

The starting and finishing position is Fudo Dachi; the time to be taken by a beginner in completing the Kata and effecting all the techniques correctly is approximately thirty seconds. A Shodan would be expected to complete all techniques correctly in about eighteen

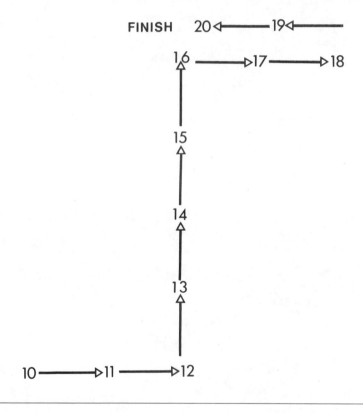

seconds – a 3rd Dan or above would be expected to complete each Kata in about ten to twelve seconds.

Taikyoku I is shown in the following sequence of photographs.

Pinan Katas I–V

The five Katas, together with the three Taikyokus, Sanchin and Tensho, provide the foundation of good Karate technique, upon which the student wishing to progress to expert ability can build. Mas Oyama Shihan has stated that these Kata exercises can be compared to the letters of the alphabet, in that, as letters are building-blocks of words and sentences, so in Karate terms these fundamental Katas are the building-blocks from which Karate is constructed.

There is not enough space to show the Pinan Katas, but the authors wish to show one advanced Kata, the Saifa Kata, the importance of which is the variety of stances and speeds employed in the Kata.

ADVANCED KATA: SAIFA

Here follows Saifa in photo form →

3 Open eyes.

4–5 Throw hands up and pull down with method. Before hands come down,

1 Stand in ready stance.

2 Move into Musubi Dachi, eyes closed.

oth hands in usual Ibuki breathing
nove on to toes and balls of both feet.

6 Complete Ibuki breathing.

7 Step forward at 45° angle on right foot.

8 Bring left foot to right. Put clenched right fist into palm of left hand.

11 Left hand covers at waist height. Right hand simultaneously completes an inverted fist strike.

12 Step forward with left foot about 135°.

9 Retaining right fist in left hand, snap right elbow up.

13 Place left fist in palm of right hand. Bring right foot to left. You are now facing the opposite way to the position in 8.

10 Step to side with left foot into Horse Stance, begin to cover with left hand open.

14 Lift left elbow with snap movement.

15 Commence right hand open cover. Take step to side with right foot into Horse Stance.

16 Execute left hand inverted fist strike. Right hand covers to waist.

19   20

17–21 Take a further right foot step forward at the same diagonal angle as in 7. Effect the movements detailed in 8–11 above.

22 Take a quick step to the left with left foot. The right foot is turned to point to the right. Look to the right.

21

23–4 Bring the right foot towards the left, slowly. Commence a downward curved block with the right hand, and an upward block with the left hand.

27 Execute a middle kick to the front, and bring foot back.

28 Take a step to the side with the right foot. The left foot is turned to face to the left. Look to the left.

25 Complete the leg and hand
movements. The heel of the right
hand pushes down.

26 Snap the head to the front.

29–31 Execute the same movements with opposite hands and the left leg
as in 23–27.

31

32 Take a long step to the rear with the left foot. Throw out both hands palms up in a grabbing movement.

35 Open both hands.

36 Swing both hands downwards in a wide circle.

33–4 Pull hands back to punching position, and execute a quick double punch forward at head height.

37 Clench the left fist before hands strike.

38 Hands strike at approximate navel height.

39 Step across with the right foot and get ready to pivot.

40 Turn to face reverse way and thrust hands out, palms upward; in a similar grabbing movement to 32.

43–4 Effect a downward circle with hands similar to 36.

41 Pull back to punching position, fists made up.

42 Execute a double punch to head height.

45 Clench the right fist before hands strike.

46 The right fist strikes the open left hand.

47 Get ready to reverse back to the original direction. Begin by sweeping the right foot along the floor until it is slightly in front of the left foot.

48 Pivoting 90° on the left leg, lift the right knee high and stamp the right foot down in Sanchin Stance.

51 Open the right hand and execute a hooking movement with it.

52 Pull the right hand back to the punching position and simultaneously execute a left inverted forefist middle thrust.

49 Swing the right hand over the head to strike a hammer fist blow.

50 Pull the left hand back to the punching position, complete hammerfist blow and shout (Kiai) loudly.

53–61 Steps 47–52 are repeated but in reverse position.

55   56

59 Pivot on the leftfoot 135° to
reverse direction. The right hand
extended in open knife hand position.
The stance is the Back Leaning Stance.

60 Pull the right hand towards chin,
simultaneously open the left hand
into a spear hand and thrust this
forward at waist height.

57 Step forward with the right
foot into the Forward Leaning
Stance. Simultaneously execute
a forefist middle thrust.

58 Take a step diagonally to the
right with the left foot.

61–4 Execute rotating two hands block.

63

64

67

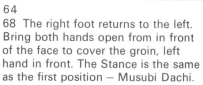

68 The right foot returns to the left. Bring both hands open from in front of the face to cover the groin, left hand in front. The Stance is the same as the first position — Musubi Dachi.

65 Pull both hands back in open position.

66 Execute a double open hand strike, with Ibuki.

FREE STYLE FIGHTING
and PRE-ARRANGED FIGHTING

Jiyu Kumite (free style fighting or sparring) is the most advanced of the forms of fighting practised in Karate.

Actual striking of blows, particularly to the head and genitals, is prohibited. At high-grade level, nevertheless, amongst grades of equal rank, punches and kicks are frequently delivered to the body, and leg sweeps and trips are carried through, in order to simulate as far as possible the likely circumstances of actual combat. As a high degree of control over blows and undue exuberance is necessary to prevent injury, the senior grades in the school will lead the lower grades into free style fighting and control ill-governed aggression by hot-tempered students and those wishing to misuse their greater size and strength.

There is a great difference between *Budo* Karate free fighting, where there are no rules, and competition or 'sport' Karate fighting. It is generally accepted that good competition fighters are not necessarily good street fighters. There are some Karateka, however, who have both the speed reflexes and control required to make a good competition fighter and also the power, strength and presence of mind not only to deliver a damaging blow but even to take the one that gets through. It cannot be denied that the peak of Karate fighting ability is to attain a high standard of Budo Karate free fighting and also a high proficiency within the confines of competition rules of free fighting.

In its physical manifestation, Karate is primarily a system of weaponless fighting, and the achievement of a high ability in free fighting is the essential heart in the Karate body. Without the development of such an ability, Karate would become little more than shadow boxing or a game for one person.

Proficiency in free fighting will not be obtained by simply attempting to practise controlled combat technique. A thorough understanding of and a high degree of ability in basic techniques, and particularly in Katas, is necessary before the student finds that he will have the balance and techniques to enable him to take part in free fighting with sufficient control of his strength and body weight. Many hours of hard work must be put in on basic techniques and the perfection of techniques in movement and Katas, and then the student must begin to develop a very necessary sense of timing and distance.

Calculating the opponent's intentions from reading his total movements and from studying his eyes, and controlling his own breathing and expressions to give nothing away, are all points which must be studied and perfected by the student who is entering the period of his Karate training when free fighting becomes of paramount importance.

FORMS OF PRE-ARRANGED FIGHTING

There are two principal methods of pre-arranged fighting which lead the student progressively to free fighting (Jiyu Kumite). These two methods are called by different names in different styles but are normally understood by the descriptions three-step sparring (Sambon Kumite) and one-step sparring (Ippon Kumite).

In both Ippon and Sambon Kumite, one person will assume the role of the attacker and his partner that of defender. Both persons will

138

understand what the other will be doing, i.e. the movements are totally pre-arranged. In both these forms of Kumite, the object is to aid the student to progress from basic techniques practised as a form of shadow boxing, into situations where he develops an awareness of an opponent who can either strike first or retaliate. The steps in the progression are through commencement of movement and the attainment of rhythm and co-ordination.

In three-step sparring, there will be three steps and three similar pre-determined attacks by the student who has been instructed to attack. The defender will defend against the three attacks and will retaliate after covering or blocking the third attack. In one-step sparring, there is one attack only; there is, therefore, less time for the defender to consider his retaliation.

The students should play alternately the part of the attacker and the defender.

EXAMPLES OF THREE-STEP SPARRING

Ready Position

Attacker in Zenkutsu Dachi

Parry with Foot and retaliate with side kick.

Parry with outer block and retaliate with Uraken strike.

Parry with reverse arm. Finally take attacking arm across body for arm break

Attacker in Zenkutsu Dachi

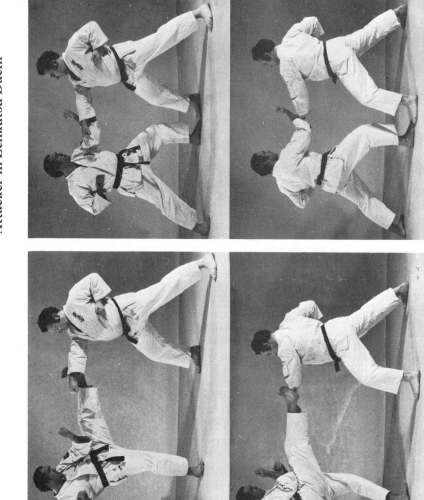

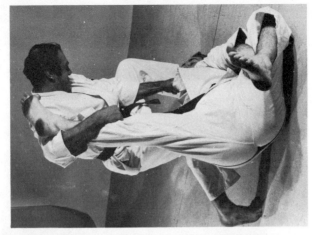

Outside block against arm. After third block move towards attacker lifting forward leg; follow down with punch with left arm

Outside block using foot. Retaliate with roundhouse kick to face with non-blocking leg.

EXAMPLES OF
ONE-STEP SPARRING

Attacker Assumes Zenkutsu Dachi Position

Block with open hand block.

Block strong punch at head with open
double arm block.

Upper thrust attack, block with rising
block.

Step up and to side of attacker and strike with roundhouse knee attack; or . . . .

Reply to attack with kick to attacker's groin.

Retaliate with finger strike to attacker's eyes; or . . . .

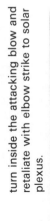

turn inside the attacking blow and retaliate with elbow strike to solar plexus.

with palm strike to jaw.

Block upper punch with rising block and pull attacking arm down with a circular movement.

Block with Koken (wrist) and retaliate with wrist strike to attacker's face.

In the following attacks the attacks are made with the left arm.

Block inside the blow, then use the blocking wrist to hook the opponent's arm and pull forward. Finally lock the elbow with the right arm and strike to the attacker's face with left hand . . . .

Duck very quickly under attacking arm and unbalance attacker with push movement from left hand and a strong pull from the right hand.

As the attacker falls, control the leg which has been hooked.

Still controlling the leg, strike to the groin with side foot kick.

to eyes . . .

Strike with left hand with one knuckle fist.

or to side of head with thumb knuckle fist.

STANCES FOR FREE FIGHTING

The purpose of and technical detail on classical Karate stances have already been explained. In Jiyu Kumite, the emphasis is not on technical perfection in positioning, but rather on more practical considerations, particularly mobility, tempered by the personal preferences and experience of the individual student.

A student must consider and attempt all the suggested fighting stances in this book, but obviously he will develop greater strength, facility and mobility in one stance. Like a soldier, however, he must be able to use all weapons at his disposal even though he will almost certainly develop a preference for and confidence in a particular weapon.

All stances can be used in free fighting, but all have particular weaknesses. The authors' intention is to refer to the main stances found in competition and to draw the reader's attention to the particular weaknesses of the stances illustrated.

Fighting Kiba Dachi (Horse Stance)
This stance will be shorter than in the classical technical stance. It is very strong for thrusting punches and can be used for taking an extra long stride and striking Jun Tsuki (side thrust punch).
The disadvantage of this stance is that although very strong and solid, it is not a mobile stance and can leave the back weak and unprotected.

148

Fighting Kokutsu Dachi (Back
Leaning Stance)
Less strong than the first stance
described above, its advantage is that
it allows the Karateka to shift the
body weight forward and back very
rapidly. In fact, it is probably the most
mobile of the fighting stances from a
rapid movement and repositioning
standpoint.

A further advantage is that kicks can
be effected from both the front and
back legs without the body weight
having to be substantially shifted.
The very short stance similar to
Kokutsu Dachi, namely Neko Ashi
Dachi (Cat Stance), whilst again a
very mobile stance, particularly for
small people against larger heavier
opponents, suffers from the problem
that the legs and feet are very close
together and, therefore, the Karateka in such a position is vulnerable to
heavy leg sweeps.

Fighting Zenkutsu Dachi (Forward Leaning Stance) Probably the most widely used stance in competition because of its good general manoeuvrability and its facility for delivering a fast Mae Geri (forward kick) and Gyaku Tsuki (reverse thrust punch) which are two of the most popular competition techniques.
The fighting stance is shorter than the classical stance, but does not allow a kick to be effected by the leading foot without shifting the body weight back.

In recent competition, a form of Zenkutsu Dachi purely for competition purposes has been developed, with some success, primarily by the Shukokai group. This stance with a predominant forward lean allows the Karateka rapid forward movement in attack, but the authors would suggest that it is otherwise of limited benefit. The extremely fast forward movement tends to run the attacker onto the retaliatory strikes of the defender, often with damage being caused to the attacker. The result of this in competition is that the defender is then often disqualified for insufficient control or striking the opponent, and this situation is now being considered to see whether the rules may need modification in the circumstances described.

In Jiyu Kumite, the individual Karateka will adopt the stance which best suits his individual physical characteristics and strengths – length of leg, body weight, etc., and his own temperament – primarily an attacking or a defensive posture.

POSITION OF HANDS

Normally, the left hand will be held in front and used mainly for deflecting or warding off the opponent's attacks; the right hand will be closer to the body (but usually slightly in front of it) and will principally be used for attacking with a punching technique. If the reader is left-handed, the position of the hands will be reversed.

The height at which the hands should be held will depend on, in the case of the right hand, the inclination and attacking technique of the individual – and, in the case of the left hand, the person's assessment of the likely area of attack by the opponent.

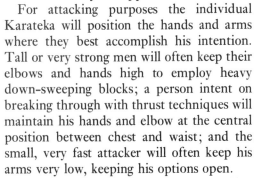

For attacking purposes the individual Karateka will position the hands and arms where they best accomplish his intention. Tall or very strong men will often keep their elbows and hands high to employ heavy down-sweeping blocks; a person intent on breaking through with thrust techniques will maintain his hands and elbow at the central position between chest and waist; and the small, very fast attacker will often keep his arms very low, keeping his options open.

Since both hands can be used for blocking and attacking, and both should be so used, the forward arm will usually cover the top half of the body, and the arm closer to the body will normally cover the lower part of the body. The general principle is that the arms should be held in such a position and with such amount of strength that they can take the impact of a blow without allowing the blow to go through to the body, and at the same time are at a sufficient distance to allow a full blow to be delivered against the opponent.

As with the eyes, the hands can be trained to deceive and mislead the opponent into making a wrong assessment of a likely attack, and many good competition fighters will continually shift the position of the hands and arms to upset and frustrate the opponent's attack.

GLIMPSES FROM CONTEST AND JIYU KUMITE

Concentration and anticipation by both contestants. Feet well positioned and balanced for quick movement — hands well placed.

Contestant on the right attacking is not on strong balance, the left contestant is in good position to take advantage as in the next photograph.

A fast drop reverse punch. (*Photo by Tony Fisher*)

Both contestants well placed but both with noticeably low hand positions leaving face vulnerable to a quick roundhouse kick.

A fine example of a good roundhouse kick to the jaw where the opponent's hands have been kept very low.

Both contestants well placed and scoring simultaneously. (*Photo by Tony Fisher*)

ANCILLARY
and ADVANCED TRAINING

In addition to the practice of basic techniques, the study, practice and attainment of expertise in Kata and the various forms of pre-determined fighting and free fighting, other important areas of training must be considered.

Apart from general conditioning, running and outdoor training, ancillary Karate training falls principally into the following groups:

(a) Use of training equipment
(b) Hand conditioning and the use of the Makiwara
(c) Tameshiwara

USE OF TRAINING EQUIPMENT

This includes the use of barbells, dumbells and other standard weight-lifting equipment, but particularly sandbags and punchballs.

The authors do not propose to set out in this book the arguments for and against the use of weights. Suffice it to say that all serious sports-men, from track and field athletes to table tennis players, make use of the benefits obtainable from weight training. For Karate purposes, the intention of weight training should be to increase strength and not to produce the very large and bulky muscles of the body-builder. Therefore, low repetitions should be employed with the maximum poundage which can be borne by the student.

A note of caution must be introduced when advocating the use of weights. Massive bodies *per se* are of dubious benefit in the world of Karate, but power aligned with speed, plus the ability to utilise that power to the maximum, makes for a formidable opponent. Thus for each period spent by the Karate student increasing his strength by using the weights, at least two sessions, each of equal length and concentration, should be spent on basic Karate training with the emphasis on speed techniques.

The standard strength-increasing exercises used by all athletes, with barbell or a pair of dumbells, are quite suitable for assisting the Karate student. These should normally comprise bench press, military press from the shoulders, arm curls, dead lift from the floor and bent-over rowing. Low repetition squats should also be introduced.

The exercises with weights shown at the end of the third chapter are specifically for the purpose of strengthening certain Karate movements.

The use of training bags and punchballs is of great importance to the Karate student. Bag training is employed primarily to obtain a sense of speed and timing. The bag can be fixed in such a way that it does not actually move when struck, although naturally it gives with the strike, or alternatively suspended in such a way that it will swing freely from its support, enabling the student to move to and fro with the swing. Bags are of special value to beginners as they allow the student to strike at a semi-hard surface which has sufficient give not to damage the fist or other striking surface should it be badly formed.

The authors realise that some clubs do not have the space nor the facilities for suspended bags. Some of the techniques shown against bags have, therefore, been photographed with one student holding a bag at different heights to enable the other to effect punches, kicks, etc., against the bag. In this case, the student holding the bag will at least be able to practise and develop strength in certain stances.

157

Chudan Tsuki

Uraken

→

The punch bag is particularly suitable for the practice of elbow techniques as the elbows are sensitive to striking against a hard surface. In using the elbow, which is a close-quarter weapon, the timing required to co-ordinate the hip, upper body and arm movements should be carefully mastered. The bag is utilised for practising kicks as they provide large targets, give when struck and will not damage the feet or knees.

Mae Geri

Mae Geri   Mawashi Geri

Yoko Geri against a hanging bag

Mawashi Kubi Geri

HAND
CONDITIONING
AND THE USE OF
THE MAKIWARA

The makiwara is a Karate striking-board. It is made from wood and is normally about fifty-five inches high, four inches wide and about two inches thick. It is either fastened to the floor with bolts or mounted on a platform. The front area of the board is padded with straw or spongey material.

Thrusting into the padded board is an excellent way to develop power in the arm, wrist and hip. It is invaluable for developing proper focus.

Striking Chudan Tsuki in Zenkutsu Dachi stance

Completed thrust in Zenkutsu Dachi

Arm held incorrectly

The strike should be done about twenty times with each arm. The Forward Leaning Stance is normally used. It is important to gauge the distance to the board; the abdomen is tensed immediately prior to the strike, and the hips and legs add additional power.

After striking, the hand and hips return to the original position. The whole movement is done as quickly as possible, but with control. The student, to prevent damage to the hand, should try to ensure that the fist is correctly formed and the thrust and stance are technically correct, before speeding up the movement.

left: A bad strike, the arm is loose and incorrectly torqued

Wrist held incorrectly

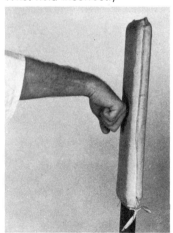

162

top and bottom left: Shuto training

Uraken training

The makiwara board is used also for training the front, roundhouse and side kicks. *(left)*.

Roundhouse kick (Mawashi Geri) against the makiwara. This kick is effected from the side of the board. The two photographs show the same kick directly to the board from in front *(right and bottom left)*.

Mae Geri: Note how the hands are held in a controlled position *(below right)*.

Yoko Geri against
the makiwara

Most Karate schools fall
into one of two groups when
the subject of conditioning
of hands, primarily by the
use of the makiwara, is con-
cerned. Some schools advo-
cate heavily conditioned
hands. These 'hard hand'
schools are now in the
minority, but will normally
insist that their Karate is the
'true' variety. The majority
of schools, however, now
contend that moderate
hand-conditioning is all that
is required in modern con-
ditions. Indeed, due to the
risk in later life of the limita-
tion in the use and move-
ment of the hands and even
the suffering of degenerative
arthritis, the painful and
lengthy callousing of the
hands advocated by the
'hard hand' schools should
only be considered seriously
by students proposing a
professional career in the
art.

In the past, when Karate
was used in actual combat, toughening of the hands was required to
break through the wooden armour of the Samurai. Such heavily conditioned hands are not considered by the authors as being necessary

165

today. However, from a standpoint of efficiency, if the only objective is to cause the maximum penetration and damage to the opponent for military or other acceptable purposes, the conditioning of the striking surface allied to the other Karate essentials of speed and power is a necessity. In such a case, considerable makiwara training would be introduced progressively to the student by the instructor.

TAMESHIWARA

Tameshiwara means 'test of breaking' and contrary to popular belief is not performed for exhibitionism. To the experienced practitioner, breaking tests his ability to transmit effective power. To the student who has been trained for some little time only, say nine to twelve months, breaking under supervision will indicate his progress and give him confidence.

The expert, in order to show how the direction of the focus of power can be transferred, will arrange (normally) for

Shuto break

boards to be placed in front and behind him, and to his left and right. The boards will then be broken in very rapid succession with different hand and foot techniques.

Criticism can be, and often is, levelled at the schools of Karate which practise breaking on the grounds that it is nothing more than flashy showmanship and panders to the element of destructiveness present in most people. Certainly, the intention of displays of breaking given in public by experts is to attract attention, but not to give the impression that breaking is part of Karate, which it is not, but simply to demonstrate the enormous power which can be generated by the body with the correct application of the principles of Karate.

To the individual, the tests of breaking, whether effected by the fist, edge of the hand, hammerfist, elbow or foot, can be the severest mental as well as physical tests that the Karate student will experience in his Karate life. The mental concentration required to succeed on the progressively harder tests of breaking is considerable. One must be able to clear the mind completely and concentrate solely on the object to be broken.

TECHNICAL PRINCIPLES OF BREAKING

Breaking techniques are usually exhibited using wood, roofing tiles, bricks, slabs made of cinder pumice or clay, blocks of ice, and occasionally stones.

The parts of the body used to strike the object will be principally the fist (Seiken and Uraken), the side of the hand, the elbow, the ball, heel and side of the foot, and the head.

The amount of force required to break a wooden board depends on the material of the board, its shape (i.e. width, length and thickness) and the speed of the blow. The easiest shaped board to break will be very short in the line of the grain and wide at right-angles to the grain. Care must be taken in selecting boards for breaking. Some woods can never be broken and any attempt to do so will result in damage to the striking surface and considerable embarrassment if the attempted breaking is being made at a public show. Wood for breaking should be kept dry; thoroughly damp wood is practically impossible to break. Pine is the wood normally used in breaking, as it has a wide grain and is a brittle wood. The standard piece of wood will be a one-inch-thick board measuring twelve inches in both length and width. Experts who

keep their hands and feet well-conditioned for breaking will, in breaking competitions, break up to four of such boards with the fist and up to seven with the elbow.

Breaking with the Fist

The correct way to hold boards
The board will be supported at both ends and will 'bend' at the point of impact.
It will break when the force applied to it has caused it to deflect until it exceeds the wood's elastic limit and the fibres on the furthest side pull apart.

Judging the distance

The strike

Speed is an important factor in breaking. Beginners should usually use a downward strike to gain confidence, as the normal arm movement is up and down as opposed to forward and back. Dead weight alone can break a 'supported' board, that is a board (or other object) held immovable until the strike has been completed. Most breaking is 'supported' breaking. 'Non-supported' breaking is a greater test of skill because, to break the object, it will be necessary to strike with sufficient speed that the inertia at the ends of the object remains effectively just behind the central impact point. If, say, a board suspended from a string is struck without the necessary speed, then the whole board will accelerate away from the striking force. Dead weight alone can break a 'supported' object in the same way as force from a strike, but it cannot break the 'unsupported' object without the requisite speed.

At many demonstrations, instead of wooden boards, the Karateka performing the breaking technique will use clay bricks or blocks. These tend to impress the audience but in fact are not necessarily more difficult to break. Such objects are very brittle and break on the side of the

169

strike as opposed to the actual point of impact. Wood is more elastic and consequently bends further, so requiring more penetration. Breaking bricks and blocks is, however, a measure of the ability of the breaker to exert considerable power or force at the required time.

In breaking, good co-ordination of the body is needed, requiring proper hip, head and arm movement in order to generate *speed*; the body, although loose to obtain the necessary speed to break, must

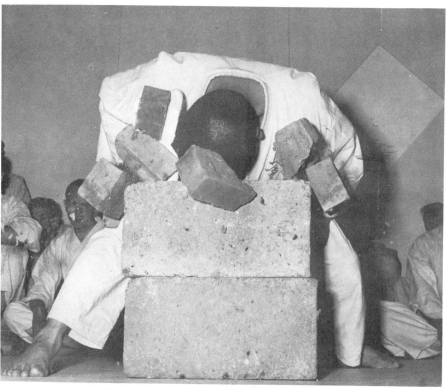

A tremendous break with the head

tighten into a single rigid power-unit just prior to the instant of striking.

The greater the number of boards that are placed together, obviously, the greater the resistance, as each board has to bend until it snaps and the total force is, therefore, multiplied by the number of boards.

170

Breaking with Shuto

Breaking with front kick

Breaking with roundhouse kick

It is harder, however, to break a *single* board as thick as the several boards placed together. The force required to break the one board is more than needed to break a number of boards of the same thickness. The force required to break a number of boards placed together will be reduced if a space is left between each layer of wood.

Breaking with side kick

Extinguishing a candle with a punch.   The candle flickers . . .
                                               . . . The candle goes out.

KARATE ETIQUETTE

As we have seen from Funakoshi's teaching, etiquette is stressed in Karate teaching at least as much as in the other martial arts. The rigid dojo discipline, the insistence by masters of each style that their students comply with the accepted etiquette of the style, and the utilisation of the term *Karate-do* – or *way* of Karate – to emphasise the ethical basis of this system of self-defence, are all evidence of matters which differentiate Karate and other martial arts – but particularly Karate – from 'sport' in the accepted sense of the word.

The Western world has produced many fighting arts, but these have rarely, if ever, included a philosophy in the art itself. Karate-*do* infers not only the necessity for the student to learn the physical application of technique, but also the spiritual utilisation of such techniques towards self-realisation and self-fulfilment. Many martial arts, including Karate, also have a religious foundation, and a shrine will be found in the major dojos at their highest point as a reminder of Karate's philosophical background. A further reminder is the period left for meditation (Zazen), usually at the end of the training session, to clear the mind and to relax the body.

THE KARATE DOJO

Karate is taught in a school called a dojo. The senior dojo instructor will be known as the *Sensei*, if a 3rd Dan or above, or *Sempai*, if a 2nd Dan or below. In a Chinese dojo (Kwoon) the senior instructor will be called Sifu, which is a term of great honour. *Sensei* literally means 'honourable teacher' and the phrase is used to denote persons in certain professions, medicine, law, etc., and is therefore not limited to the Karate world.

(Photo by Paul von Stroheim)

The chief master or instructor of a style or system will be known as *Shihan*. At one time in most schools the Sensei lived in or in premises adjoining the dojo.

(Photo by Paul von Stroheim)

THE BOW OR SALUTATION

The students in the dojo bow to the Sensei before and after each training session.

(a) Kneeling bow

The bow is about 30°. Note the position of the fists.

(b) Standing bow

The bow is effected in the Fudo Dachi stance. The intention is to 'see'
the whole of the opponent at the same time. The eyes should look at the
opponent's chest.

177

THE KARATE GI

The Gi, or practice suit, consists of a jacket, trousers and belt. It goes without saying that the Gi should be kept clean and repaired at all times.

The Karate Gi laid out.

178

First fold in the sleeves, then the
jacket to the centre.

Tie with belt in the same way as
tying method in next photo group.

Roll very tight.

Completed.

TYING THE BELT (OBI)

Place belt at waist leaving good lengths on each side.

Wind belt round waist and bring both ends to front.

Bring right end under left end
and other layer and pull firm.

Take left end over right and pull
tight. The knot is a reef knot.

THE BELT SYSTEM AND GRADE
TERMINOLOGY

Below black belt, members are *Kyu* grades (literally 'boy') and, depending upon the continent and school rules, will normally wear different colours for each Kyu grade, other than black.

Above the colour/belts, the grades are *Dan* grades (literally 'man') and in Kyokushinkai are as follows:

1st dan	Shodan ⎫		Sempai grades
2nd dan	Nidan ⎪		
3rd dan	Sandan ⎬ Black Belt		3rd–6th Dan
4th dan	Yondan ⎪		Sensei grade
5th dan	Godan ⎭		
6th dan	Rokudan ⎫ Red and White		
7th dan	Sichidan ⎬ Stripe Belt		Shihan
8th dan	Hachidan ⎭ Red Belt		Kyoshi grade

182